EXOSKELETON

by Kristin Cashore

PEARSON

Scott
Foresman

DK

What You Already Know

Animals can be divided into vertebrates and invertebrates.

A vertebrate is an animal with a backbone. An invertebrate is an animal without a backbone. Most animals are invertebrates.

The growth of every animal begins with an egg. With insects like butterflies, a larva hatches out of the egg. The larva then turns into a pupa while preparing to become an adult.

newly hatched ostrich

All animals are born with adaptations. An animal's adaptations are inherited from its parents. Behavior is an adaptation. For example, some animals are born with the instinct to migrate or to

European striped snail

hibernate during winter. A trait is a body part, type of behavior, or ability to learn a behavior that an animal receives from its parents.

Fossils teach us about animals that lived long ago. By studying fossils, we learn how animals have changed over time.

In this book you will learn about an invertebrate adaptation: the exoskeleton. Animals with exoskeletons are all around us. To find out more about these animals, keep reading!

Skeletons

You know what a skeleton is. But have you ever heard of an exoskeleton? What about an endoskeleton?

An exoskeleton is a hard outer covering that gives an animal strength and support. An exoskeleton protects an animal's soft inner organs. Most invertebrates have exoskeletons instead of bones to support their bodies and protect their organs.

An endoskeleton is the frame of bones inside vertebrates. This frame of bones protects their organs and supports their bodies.

tiger endoskeleton

When a pillbug is in danger, it will curl into a ball with its exoskeleton facing out.

Because most animals are invertebrates, most animals have exoskeletons. Have you ever seen a ladybug? Did you notice its hard, shiny wing covers? Or maybe you have seen the shell of a clam? The ladybug's hard covering and the clam's shell are both exoskeletons. Insects, spiders, centipedes, and millipedes have exoskeletons. So do many sea animals, such as crabs, lobsters, and shrimp.

Some animals don't have any type of skeleton! For example, jellyfish have neither an exoskeleton nor an endoskeleton. Their soft bodies can change shape freely.

A jellyfish is an invertebrate, but it does not have an exoskeleton.

Your skin expands as you grow bigger. Most exoskeletons do not expand. As an invertebrate grows, it must shed its exoskeleton and form a new one. This is called molting. Some invertebrates molt many times during their lives.

Exoskeletons are hard. Despite their hardness, most can flex in places to allow animals to move. Exoskeletons are often heavy and thick. Animals that have them tend to be small. The bodies of most vertebrates would collapse if exoskeletons were forced to support too large a body!

Animals with exoskeletons are found all over the Earth. They live on the land, in the sea, and also in streams and rivers.

Thanks to its green exoskeleton, this mantis looks like a leaf!

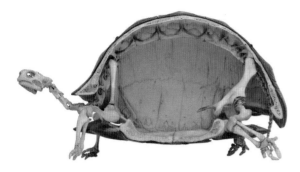

This side view of a tortoise shows both its endoskeleton and its exoskeleton.

There are two kinds of animals that have both endoskeletons and exoskeletons. Do you already know which two animals they are?

Tortoises and turtles are vertebrates. Like other reptiles, they have endoskeletons. But they also have shells. Turtles and tortoises can pull their heads, feet, and tails all the way into their shells. Their shells serve as exoskeletons, protecting them from their enemies.

The freshwater crayfish lives in streams and rivers. Crayfish have exoskeletons.

Arthropods

millipede

The word *arthropod* means "jointed foot." Arthropod bodies have different sections, and are covered by a jointed exoskeleton. The joints allow the stiff exoskeleton to bend for easier movement. Arachnids, insects, centipedes, millipedes, and crustaceans are arthropods.

The exoskeleton of an arthropod is made of a hard material called chitin. Chitin covers the arthropod's whole body, including its legs, eyes, and antennae! Arthropods molt several times before becoming adults.

The hair on a tarantula is actually part of its exoskeleton.

Arachnids

Many people think that spiders are insects. But spiders are actually arachnids!

Arachnids are arthropods. They have eight legs. Their bodies are made of two parts: the head and the abdomen. Arachnids shed their exoskeletons in order to grow.

Spiders need to rest right after shedding. But if a spider does not flex its new exoskeleton, it can become too hard. Spiders can even regrow a missing leg by shedding!

Scorpions are also arachnids. Scorpions live in warm, dry places, like deserts. They are bigger than most spiders. Some scorpions grow to be eight inches long! Scorpions have a sharp stinger at the end of their tail that helps them catch insects and small animals.

Careful! Do you see the stinger on the tail of this desert scorpion?

Insects

Insects have six legs. Their bodies have three parts: the head, the thorax, and the abdomen.

Insects' exoskeletons do the same job as the exoskeletons of arachnids. They protect and support insects. Insects stay waterproof because of their exoskeletons.

An insect's muscles attach to the inside of its exoskeleton. Insects may be tiny, but they have many, many muscles. Have you ever seen an insect carrying a piece of food many times larger than itself? Insects are strong because of their exoskeletons and muscles.

A male rhinoceros beetle uses its horns to fight with other males for a mate.

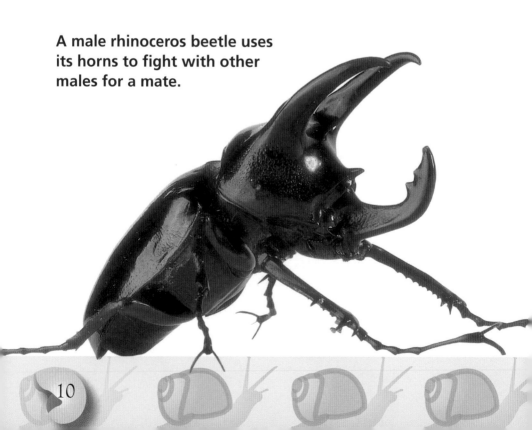

Some insects have very fancy exoskeletons. A ladybug is usually red, orange, or yellow with black spots. Their bright colors warn birds and other insects that they taste bitter. The color of their exoskeleton protects them from predators.

When this ladybug begins to fly, it opens its wing casings and stretches out its wings.

A rhinoceros beetle's exoskeleton is one of the fanciest! A male rhinoceros beetle has horns that are strong enough to pierce its rival's exoskeleton. Many beetles have spikes or horns built into their exoskeletons.

Locusts are insects that sometimes move in swarms.

Insects and Growth

Some insects go through many stages of growth before becoming adults. Insects' exoskeletons do not expand or change. Because of this, an insect cannot grow without shedding its exoskeleton.

When an insect becomes too big for its exoskeleton, the exoskeleton cracks open. The insect wriggles out and pulls away from the old exoskeleton.

Damselflies are born underwater. A young damselfly, or nymph, molts many times while it is growing underwater. Then one day, it climbs out of the water and molts for the last time. When its wings dry and its body hardens, it is an adult.

Damselfly nymph holds onto underwater stem.

Nymph sheds skin while still underwater.

After an insect has shed its exoskeleton, it can take hours or even days for its new exoskeleton to harden. During this time, the insect is soft and unprotected, and cannot move much. If the insect is lucky, it will remain safe until its new exoskeleton has formed.

The insect's new exoskeleton is bigger than the last one. It is the right shape for this new stage of the insect's life. Most insects stop molting once they are adults.

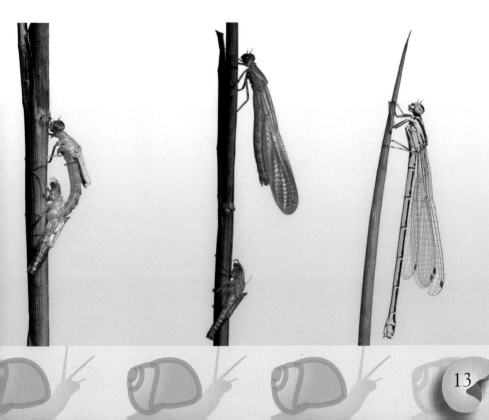

Nymph breaks away from its old skin.

Young damselfly moves out of water and continues to grow.

adult female

Sea Creatures

The oceans are full of invertebrates with exoskeletons. Many sea animals, such as the nautilus, have exoskeletons that grow into beautiful shapes. The nautilus uses its shell for protection. It also traps air in its shell, which helps it float in the water.

Water is much thicker than air. It gives more support to sea animals. Because of this, sea animals with exoskeletons can grow bigger than animals with exoskeletons that live on the land.

Echinoderms, crustaceans, and mollusks are all sea animals that have exoskeletons. Echinoderms include starfish and sea urchins. Crustaceans include crabs, lobsters, and shrimp. Mollusks include clams, mussels, and oysters.

Let's take a look at what each of these groups is like, and how each group uses its exoskeleton.

A nautilus is a mollusk.
Its shell makes a very
strong exoskeleton!

A shrimp is
a crustacean.

Echinoderms

The word *echinoderm* (ik-EYE-nuh-derm) means "spiny skin." An echinoderm has a soft body that is protected by a tough exoskeleton. The exoskeleton is made of a hard material called calcite. The exoskeleton is often spiny and covered by a thin skin.

Starfish are echinoderms. Starfish have tiny tubes for feet. The tubes work like suction cups, and help move starfish around. Starfish also use their tubes to pry open the shells of clams or mussels. Starfish are very strong!

Starfish usually have five legs.

Sea urchins are also echinoderms. Their exoskeletons are covered with spines, which protect them from predators. The spines fit onto little bumps on the sea urchins' bodies. Sea urchins are able to rotate their spines in every direction around these bumps. Like starfish, sea urchins move by using tiny, tubelike feet.

The parts of a sea urchin are arranged around its center, like the slices of an orange.

Crustaceans

Crustaceans (kruh-STAY-shuns) are arthropods that live in the ocean. Crabs, lobsters, crayfish, shrimps, krill, and barnacles are crustaceans.

As with other arthropods, the exoskeletons of crustaceans are made of chitin. A crustacean has joints in its exoskeleton, which allows it to move around. The legs of a crustacean are narrow, with a number of flexible joints. This helps it to walk.

Some crustaceans move around a great deal. There are even crustaceans that migrate! For example, some lobsters migrate to deeper water during the winter.

The exoskeleton on the back of a velvet crab is covered with velvety fuzz.

Lobsters move in long, straight lines when they migrate. Many fishermen call this the "lobster march."

Like other arthropods, crustaceans have muscles which attach to the inside of their exoskeletons. Also like other arthropods, crustaceans must shed their exoskeletons in order to grow. Crustaceans grow to be bigger than most other arthropods because the water gives them extra support.

Look out! A lobster's claws are very strong and fast.

Mollusks

A mollusk is an animal with a soft body that usually has a shell. The shell is the mollusk's exoskeleton. Mollusks do not molt.

Some mollusks are gastropods. A gastropod usually has one big foot that helps it crawl along. It also usually has a curved shell that covers its soft body, and a head with eyes and tentacles. Snails, conches, and whelks are gastropods.

The yellow and pink mollusks are dog whelks. See the cluster of black shells? These are mussels.

Other mollusks are bivalves. Bivalves have a soft body with no head. They are protected by their shells, which are formed in two parts. A hinge holds the two parts together. Mussels, oysters, clams, and scallops are bivalves.

Scallops move by squirting water from their shells. It's a funny way of getting around! If a scallop is in danger, its shell closes quickly.

The shells of mollusks are made from a material rich in calcium. They are extremely strong and difficult to break. As a mollusk grows, its shell grows with it.

Queen scallops can grow to be three and a half inches across.

Animal Bodies Inside and Out

Every animal needs some kind of support, so that it can keep its shape, move, and protect itself. You get your support from your bones, but most animals get their support from exoskeletons. Beetles, scorpions, starfish, lobsters, snails, and oysters all have exoskeletons. Everywhere you look you can find animals with exoskeletons!

sea urchin shells

Some exoskeletons are like a hard skin, and others are shells. Some must be shed so that an animal can grow, and others grow with the animal. Some are flexible, and some don't move at all. Some are colorful, and some are dull.

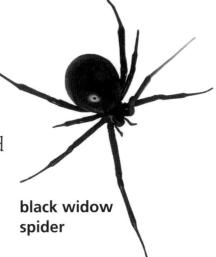

black widow spider

Exoskeletons have one thing in common. All exoskeletons are adaptations that invertebrates have. This is because exoskeletons allow most of the world's animals to live and thrive!

leaf beetle

Glossary

bivalves   mollusks with no head and a shell in two parts connected by a hinge

calcite   the hard material that forms the exoskeleton of an echinoderm

chitin   the hard material that forms the exoskeleton of an arthropod

crustaceans   arthropods that are sea creatures. A few crustaceans live in freshwater

echinoderms   sea creatures with soft inner bodies and tough outer shells

endoskeleton   the frame of bones inside a vertebrate

exoskeleton   the hard outer covering around most invertebrates

gastropod   a mollusk with one big foot, usually a curved shell, and a head with eyes and tentacles

invertebrate   an animal that does not have a backbone